MACHINES RULE!

ON THE BUILDING SITE

Steve Parker

W
FRANKLIN WATTS
LONDON • SYDNEY

This edition 2011

First published in 2008
by Franklin Watts

Franklin Watts
338 Euston Road
London NW1 3BH

Franklin Watts Australia
Level 17/207 Kent Street
Sydney, NSW 2000

Editor: Jeremy Smith
Design: Billin Design Solutions
Art director: Jonathan Hair

Picture credits: Alamy: 11all.
Shutterstock: OFC all, 2, 3, 6-7 all, 8-9 all, 11c, 12-13 all, 14-15 all, 16-17 all, 18-19 all, 20-21 all, 22-23 all, 24-25 all, 26-27 all.

A CIP catalogue record for this book is available from the British Library.

Dewey number: 629.47

ISBN 978 1 4451 0626 7

Printed in China

Franklin Watts is a division of
Hachette Children's Books,
an Hachette UK company
www.hachette.co.uk

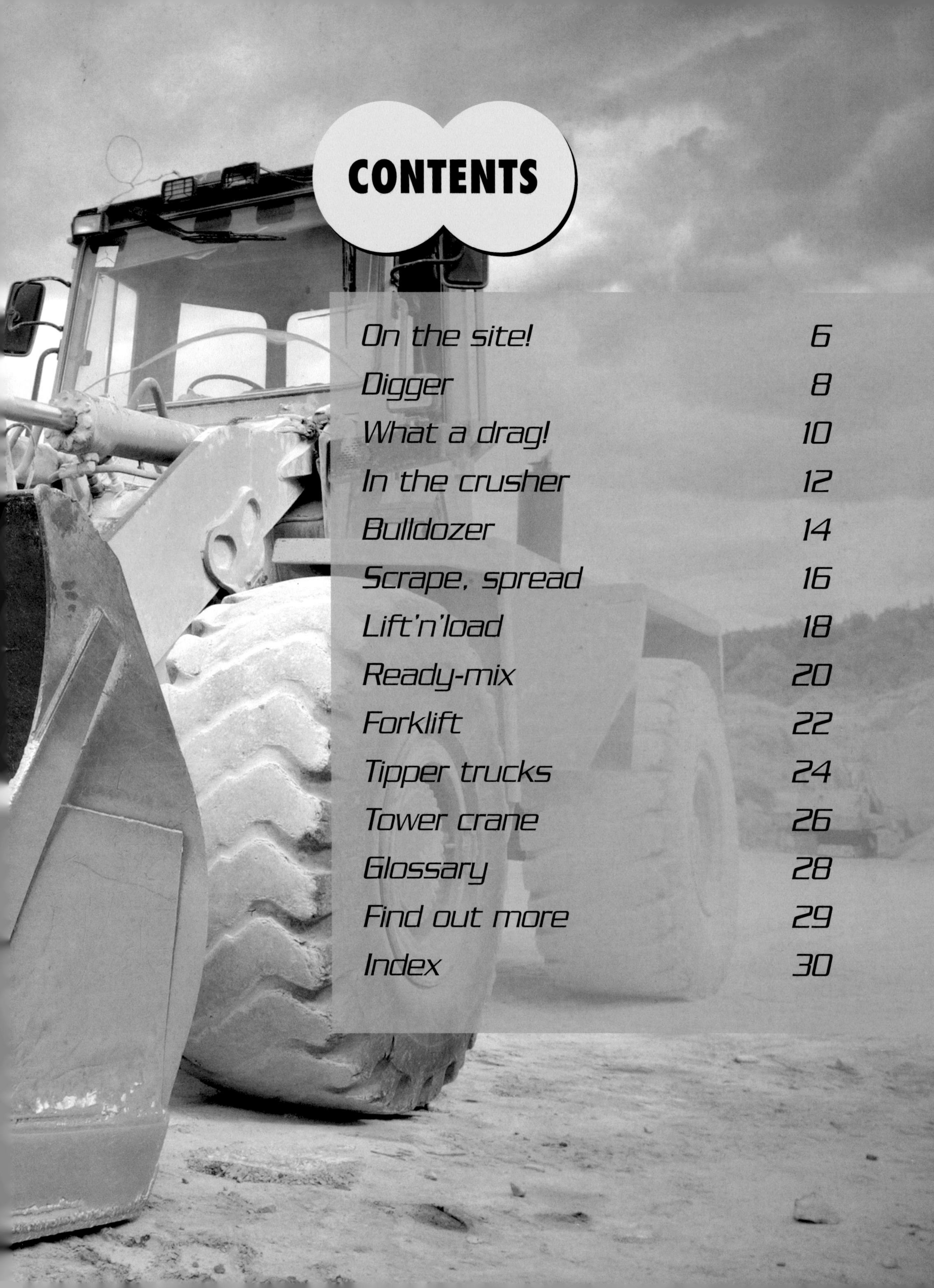

CONTENTS

On the site!

The building site is never dull. Engines roar as diggers, bulldozers and other massive machines use their strength. Trucks come and go non-stop, bringing supplies and materials. Time is money, so rain hardly slows the pace – but it does muddy the place!

Do-it-all diggers

Diggers and excavators don't just scoop earth. They lift and move loose materials such as sand, gravel, rocks and rubble, as well as packs of bricks and blocks. Like all construction machines, they are strong, tough and reliable.

Driving 'dozers

When push comes to shove, the bulldozer can't be beaten. Its shiny **blade** and crawler tracks flatten rough ground, shift piles of materials and even level out a hill.

What a dump!

Tipper and dump trucks are the workhorses of the building trade. They carry anything from muddy dirt to new doors and window frames. Loaders fill them up, and off they go again.

Bird's eye view

High in the sky, the crane operator has the best view as the building takes shape. The driver's phone is always busy with requests to move things. But it's a long way up to the **cab** – and a long way down to the toilet!

Digger

Before you start to build up – dig down! Diggers are among the first machines at a building site. They scoop out holes for a building's base, making space for the foundations or footings.

Big diggers have crawler or **caterpillar tracks**. These help to spread the huge weight and grip well in mud. You could fit six people in the digger's bucket!

THAT'S INCREDIBLE

Teams of 'dancing diggers' give shows and displays, moving to music like massive mechanical dancers.

A digger's big, tough tyres have extra-deep ridges, or **tread**, so they don't get bogged down.

Stats and Facts

JS 130L Tracked Excavator (digger)

Maker: JCB (USA)

Length: 7.6 metres, arm folded

Width: 2.7 metres across tracks

Height: 2.7 metres to top of cab

Weight: 14 tonnes

Digging height: Up to 8.8 metres

Digging forward reach: 7.97 metres

Digging depth: Down to 5.15 metres

Engine: Isuzu A4BG1T 4.33-litre turbo diesel

Speed: 5.5 km/h

Baby diggers can fit into small gardens. They shift soil 100 times faster than a person with a spade.

What a drag!

Excavators do really huge digging jobs. Dragline excavators are some of the biggest. They can have buckets as big as buses! They are used in quarries and mines, as well as for building roads and railways.

THAT'S INCREDIBLE

The world's biggest land vehicle is the Krupp Bagger 288 bucket-wheel mining excavator. It weighs 45,500 tonnes – more than many ocean liners.

The dragline excavator swings its bucket out and down on one steel cable. Then it drags the bucket back using another cable, or line, to scrape up earth.

Huge excavators are used to hollow out hills filled with valuable things such as coal, minerals and gemstones.

There are different buckets for various jobs. A narrow bucket digs, or 'hoes', a thin trench.

The wheels and cogs of giant dragline excavators must be constantly oiled to make sure they carry on working properly.

Stats and Facts

Bucyrus 8200 Walking Dragline Excavator

Maker: Bucyrus (USA)

Weight: Over 4,000 tonnes

Boom length: Up to 122 metres

Bucket size: Up to 88 cubic metres

Power: Electric motors

Load weight: Up to 170 tonnes

Dig depth: 44 metres

Dig-to-dump distance: 200 metres

Dump height: 45 metres

In the crusher

A building, road, railway or runway needs firm support underneath. The crusher breaks up lumps of stone, rock, bricks, gravel, pebbles and almost anything else, to form material for a hard, long-lasting base.

Some of the crusher's raw materials come from recycled old buildings. **Demolition** machines with grabs, claws and balls smash them apart brick by brick.

THAT'S INCREDIBLE

One giant crusher in Australia weighs 17,600 tonnes and processes 10,000 tonnes of rocks every hour.

The crusher takes in all kinds of rock-hard items at one end and pours out smaller, similar-sized bits at the other end. This rubble is great for making building materials.

Broken pieces of rock and rubble pour off the end of the crusher's **conveyor belt**.

Stats and Facts

Nordberg/Lokotrack LT1213S Mobile Crusher

Maker: Metso Nordberg (Finland)

Crusher unit: Nordberg NP1213

Feeder unit: TK11-42-2V vibrating feeder

Length for transport: 17.2 metres

Width for transport: 3 metres

Height for transport: 3.4 metres

Weight: 47.5 tonnes

Feed hopper volume: 9 cubic metres

Feed hopper size: 4.1 by 1.1 metres

Size of crushed pieces: 20–70 millimetres

Bulldozer

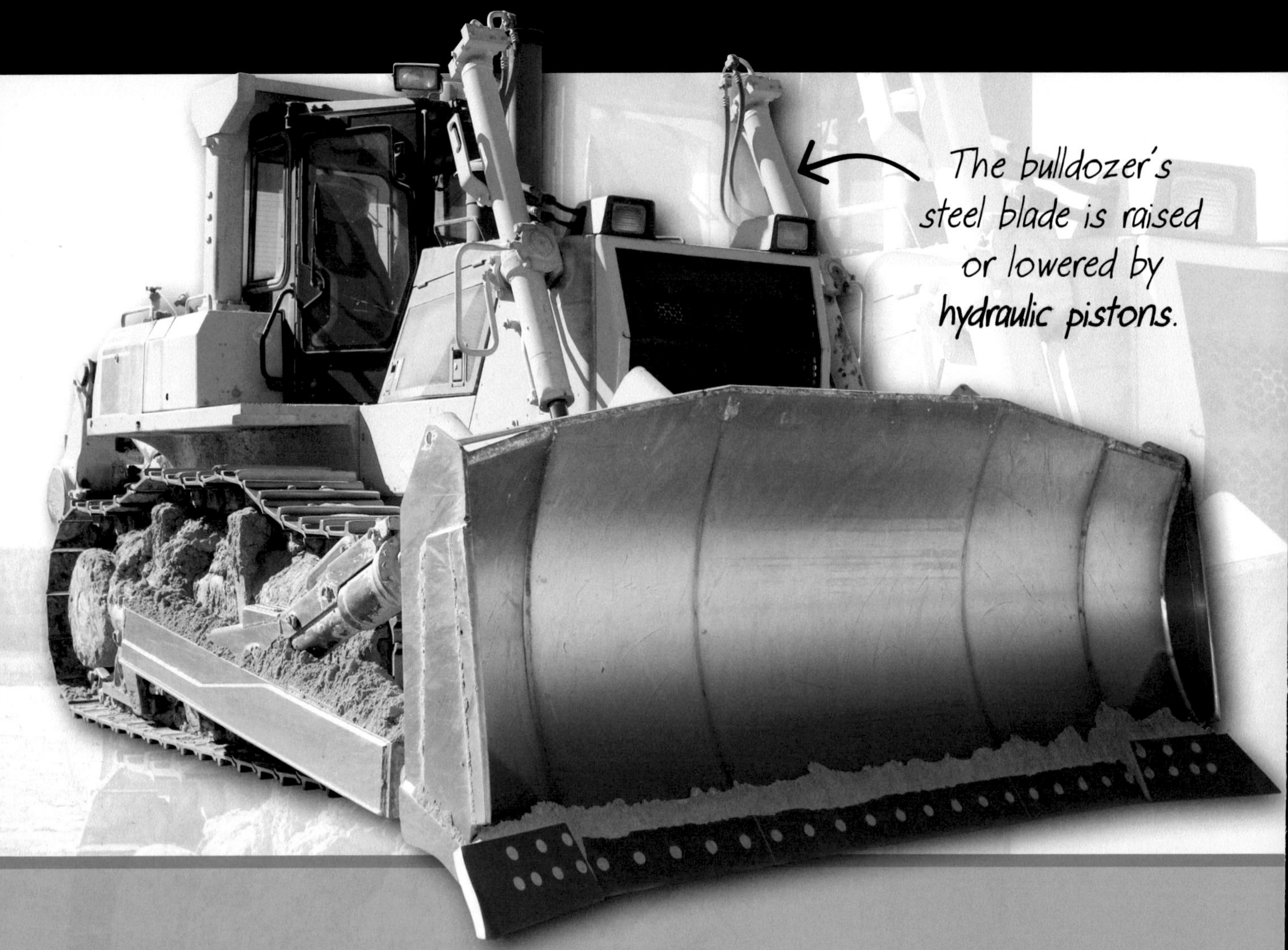

The bulldozer's steel blade is raised or lowered by **hydraulic pistons**.

If it's pushing or pulling power you need, use a bulldozer! This is the heaviest, slowest machine on many building sites. Its main job is to scrape and push surfaces flat and level.

The driver steers the bulldozer by making the caterpillar track on one side move faster than the track on the other side.

The metal ridges on the caterpillar tracks grip very well. They are moved by big cogs, which are like **gear** wheels with teeth around the edge.

Stats and Facts

Caterpillar D9

Maker: Caterpillar (USA)

Length: 8.1 metres

Blade width: 4.5 metres

Height: 4 metres

Weight: 49 tonnes

Engine: CAT C18 18-litre ACERT turbocharged diesel

Power: More than 500 horsepower

Forward speed: 12 km/h

Reverse speed: 14 km/h

THAT'S INCREDIBLE

The Komatsu D155W bulldozer works underwater, to move and flatten the sea bed around harbours and ports. This 'dozer is remote-controlled.

Some 'dozers have a claw or **ripper** at the back. As they trundle along, this tears up and loosens hard ground, even tarmac and **concrete**.

Scrape, spread

Sometimes people need a smooth area like a lawn, sports pitch, park or levelled-off building site. The land plane, leveller or scraper makes the ground as flat as a pancake.

The land plane can't push massive piles like the bulldozer. But it can make a really flat, even surface using its wide blade with adjustable height and tilt.

THAT'S INCREDIBLE

When building a new motorway, a team of land planes can level the area of a football pitch in less than two minutes.

Rollers can be used to make the ground really level.

Stats and Facts

Model 1450 Land Scraper

Maker: Leon (Canada)

Type: Towed

Length: 8.4 metres

Width: 2.94 metres

Width of cut: 2.6 metres

Weight: 5.54 tonnes

Power needs: 425 horsepower

Clearance above ground level: 26 centimetres

Depth of cut: 28 centimetres

Scrapers can be attached to most types of tractors, and are used on everything from fields to busy roads.

Lift'n'load

There are endless heavy loads to lift around a building site, from earth and rocks to bricks, blocks and pipes. The loader picks them up and carries them around.

A massive bucket scoops up loose soil, sand, gravel or rubble, a few tonnes at a time. This load is heading for the tipper truck.

This claw-like clamp picks up logs and lengths of wood.

THAT'S INCREDIBLE

The Le Tourneau L-2350 is a giant loader weighing 258 tonnes that can lift over 72 tonnes in its bucket to a height of 7.3 metres.

Stats and Facts

Volvo L120E Front Loader

Maker: Volvo (Sweden)

Length: 8 metres

Width: 2.7 metres

Height: 3.36 metres to cab roof

Weight: Up to 20 tonnes

Engine: D7D LA E2 7-litre 6-cylinder turbo diesel

Power: 224 horsepower

Bucket height: Over 4 metres

Top speed: 35 km/h

The heavy diesel engine at the back balances the load at the front, so the vehicle doesn't tip forwards.

Ready-mix

"The readymix is here, everyone grab a shovel!" When already-mixed concrete arrives, there's not a moment to lose. As soon as it's poured, it starts to harden or 'go off'. Minutes count!

The mixer contains a load of concrete. As long as the drum keeps churning around, the load will not start to go hard.

Before starting work, the mixer goes to a factory, where massive containers of sand, cement and ballast (gravel) are kept, ready to mix the next load.

Big loads of concrete pour into trenches to make firm foundations, or footings, for the main walls and girders.

A crane lifts a bulk-load bucket to the upper floors of a tall building. The concrete will flow out of the bottom.

Stats and Facts

O'Long Concrete Mixer Truck

Maker: Steyr/O'Long/Zhongtong (China)

Length: 9.13 metres

Width: 2.49 metres

Height: 3.77 metres

Weight empty: 12.8 tonnes

Engine: Weichai WD615 9.7-litres 6-cylinder petrol

Power: 360 horsepower

Drum volume: 9 cubic metres

Load weight: Up to 10.7 tonnes

Speed: 77 km/h

THAT'S INCREDIBLE

Truck-mounted concrete pumps can push the concrete up through the tube-shaped **boom** to a height of more than 60 metres.

Forklift

You probably use a 'forklift' every day – to put food in your mouth! Building sites, factories, warehouses and ports all use much bigger versions to lift and move goods around.

THAT'S INCREDIBLE

Many countries have forklift competitions that include unloading a truck in the fastest, neatest way and driving through an obstacle course.

Big diesel-engined forklifts work at ports and distribution centres. They raise standard-sized steel cargo **containers** up onto trucks, ships and railway wagons.

This is a telescopic handler, or teleporter. It has a long boom at the front that can extend forwards and upwards to reach and move loads around.

Stats and Facts

Komatsu AX20 Forklift Series

Maker: Komatsu (Japan/USA)

Length without forks: 2 metres

Width: 0.96 metres

Fork length: 1.07 metres

Fork height: Up to 5.9 metres with 3-stage mast lift

Weight: 6 tonnes

Engine: K21 4-cylinder 2.1-litre

Lift speed: 7 cm per second

Load weight: 1.4 tonnes

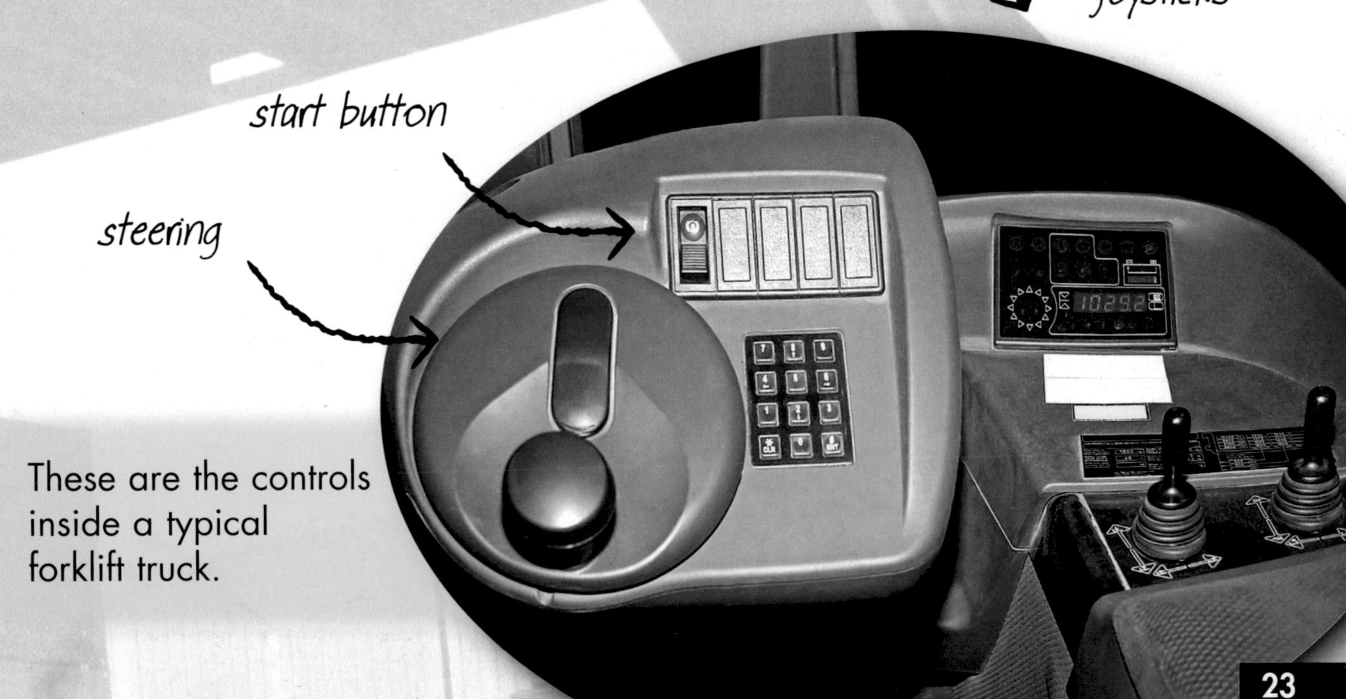

These are the controls inside a typical forklift truck.

Tipper trucks

Tipper or dump trucks come in all shapes and sizes. Some are so massive they could hold a whole house! They carry all kinds of loose materials, from clean sand to demolition debris.

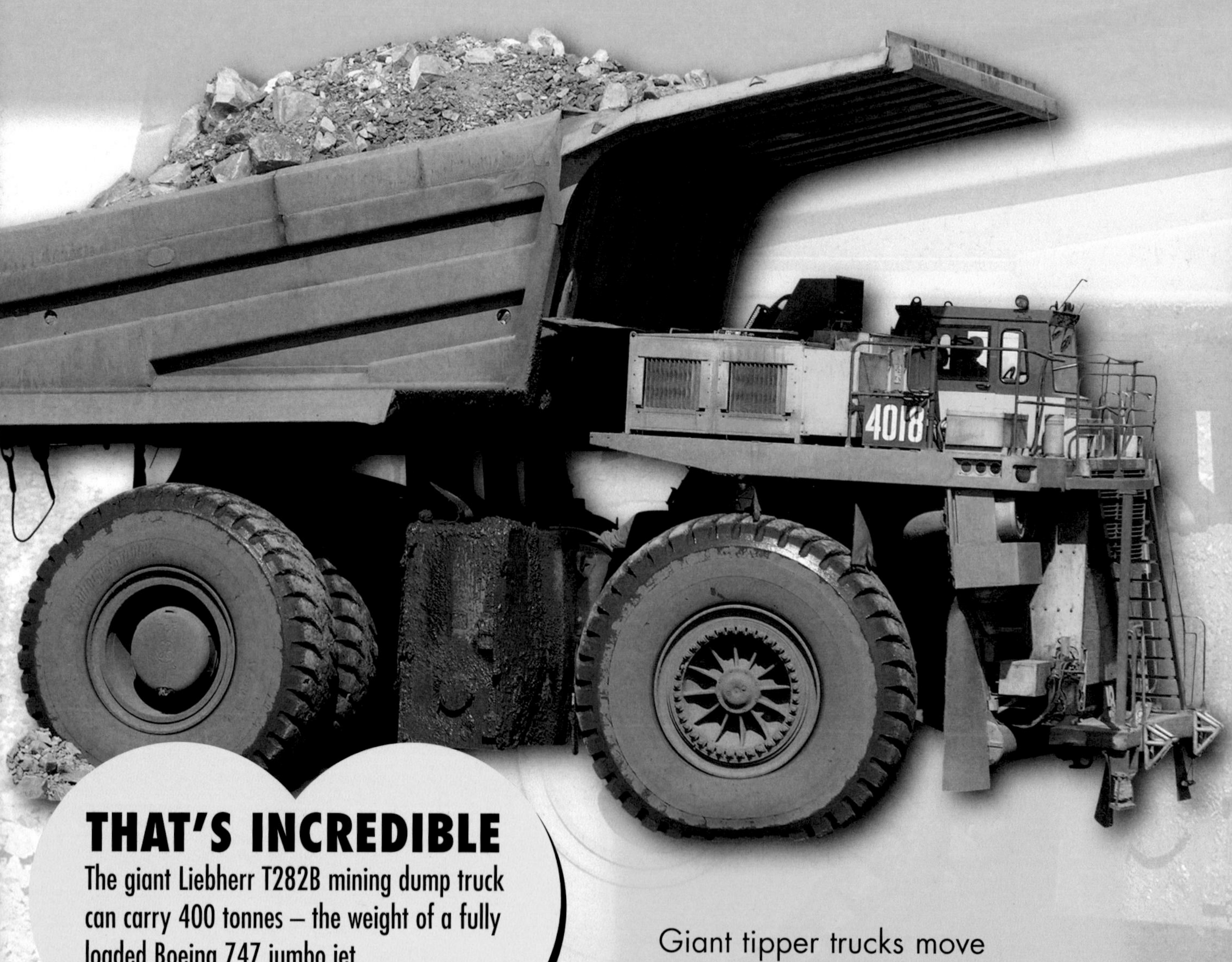

THAT'S INCREDIBLE

The giant Liebherr T282B mining dump truck can carry 400 tonnes – the weight of a fully loaded Boeing 747 jumbo jet.

Giant tipper trucks move dozens of tonnes each time. See how tiny the driver is – and all the steps up to the cab!

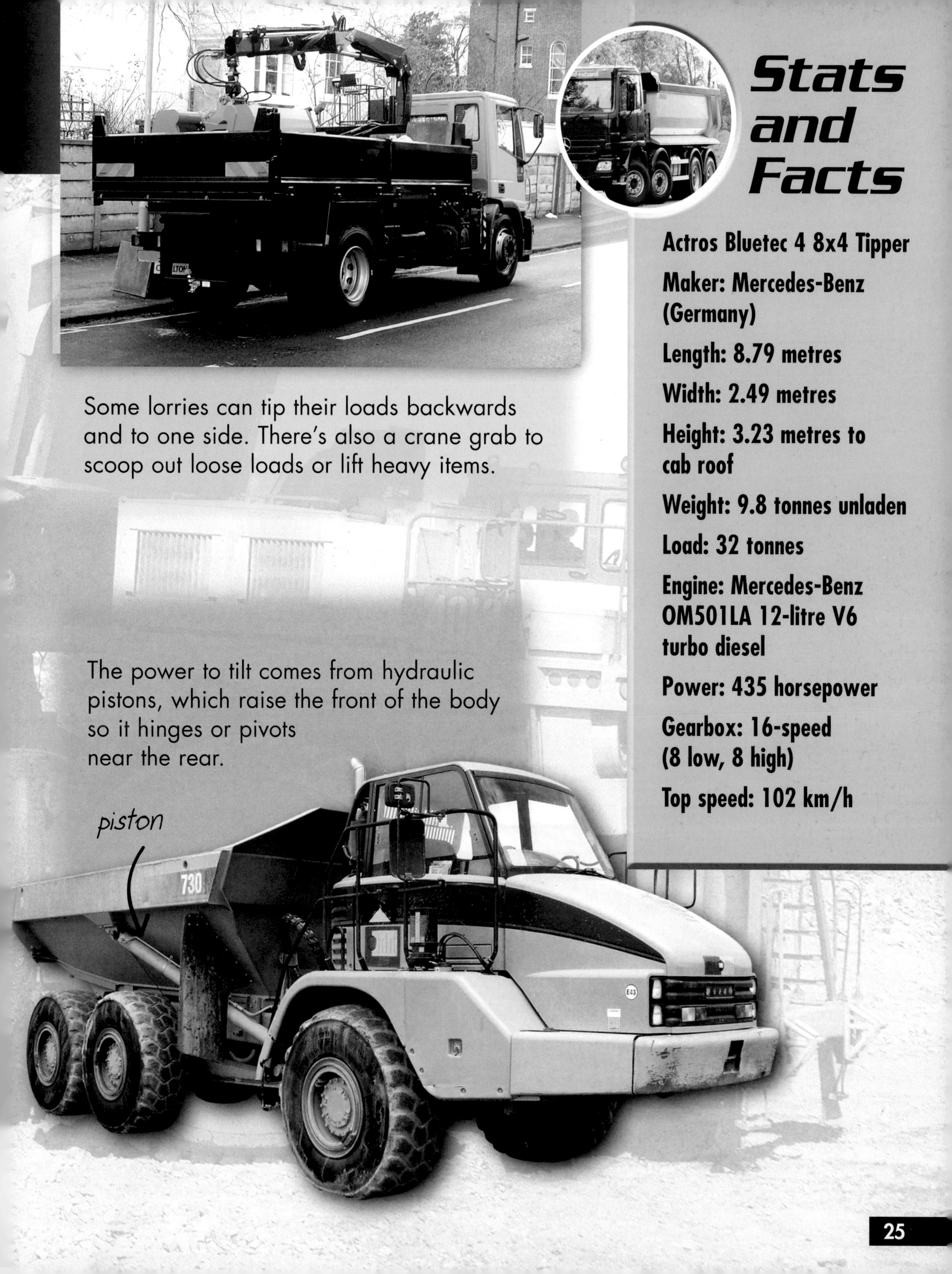

Some lorries can tip their loads backwards and to one side. There's also a crane grab to scoop out loose loads or lift heavy items.

The power to tilt comes from hydraulic pistons, which raise the front of the body so it hinges or pivots near the rear.

Stats and Facts

Actros Bluetec 4 8x4 Tipper

Maker: Mercedes-Benz (Germany)

Length: 8.79 metres

Width: 2.49 metres

Height: 3.23 metres to cab roof

Weight: 9.8 tonnes unladen

Load: 32 tonnes

Engine: Mercedes-Benz OM501LA 12-litre V6 turbo diesel

Power: 435 horsepower

Gearbox: 16-speed (8 low, 8 high)

Top speed: 102 km/h

Tower crane

For tall buildings, you need tall cranes. The tower crane is always busy on site. It lifts, swings and lowers all kinds of loads.

The crane operator has a long climb to work each day! There's a radio link for talking to people on the ground about what needs moving next.

THAT'S INCREDIBLE

The biggest tower cranes can lift and lower loads of 100 tonnes anywhere over an area of six football pitches.

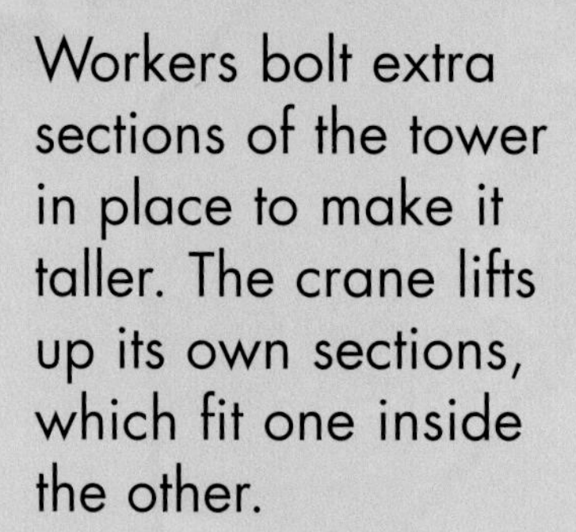

Workers bolt extra sections of the tower in place to make it taller. The crane lifts up its own sections, which fit one inside the other.

Stats and Facts

K1000 Tower Crane

Maker: Kroll (Denmark)

Total height: 120 metres

Total weight: Up to 1,000 tonnes

Tower sections: 8.5 by 12 metres

Jib length: Up to 100 metres

Load: Up to 100 tonnes standard, 250 tonnes with special equipment

Fixed counterweight: 100 tonnes

Mobile counterweights: 2 of 40 tonnes

Hoist lift speed: 50 metres per minute for 15 tonnes

The crane's long arm is the **jib.** A trolley runs along rails inside it, carrying the cable and hook. **Counterweights** at the other end stop it from toppling over.

The jib is lifted up section by section using a mobile crane (one on a truck).

Glossary

Blade
On a bulldozer, leveller or similar machine, the long smooth-edged metal part that cuts or pushes.

Boom
The long, moveable or swinging part of a big machine such as a crane or digger.

Cab
The place where a driver or operator sits to control a large vehicle, crane or similar machine.

Caterpillar track
A 'crawler' or long ridged belt in a loop shape that goes round and round, with wheels inside it, as used on tanks and big construction vehicles.

Concrete
A mix of cement, sand and small stones plus water, which 'goes off' and becomes rock-hard.

Container
Standard-sized steel box (12.2 by 2.44 by 2.59 metres) with doors at one end, which can be lifted and loaded onto trucks, ships and railway wagons.

Conveyor belt
A long, endless loop or belt that goes round and round, and carries or conveys items or materials.

Counterweight
A large, heavy block of concrete, metal or similar material that balances a vehicles load to stop it from toppling over.

Demolition
Taking apart or knocking down constructions such as houses, factories and apartment blocks.

Gears
A system of toothed wheels called cogs that come together or mesh in different combinations, inside a gearbox, so a vehicle can go at different speeds for the same engine turning speed.

Hydraulic
Working by the force of a high-pressure liquid, usually water or a special oil.

Jib
The long, arm-like part of a crane or similar machine.

Piston
A solid cylinder or disk that moves under pressure.

Ripper
A claw or claws that dig into the ground and break or rip it apart as they move along, often fixed to the back of a bulldozer.

Tread
On a tyre, the surface pattern of grooves and bumps that grip the ground.

Find out more

Websites

http://www.pbs.org/wgbh/buildingbig/skyscraper/basics.html

Part of the large Building Big site covering all kinds of huge constructions such as skyscrapers, dams, bridges and tunnels, and the machines that make them.

http://www.buildingconstructionequipment.com/Bulldozer.asp

A big site with details of many construction machines, from cranes to forklifts.

http://science.howstuffworks.com/tower-crane.htm

http://science.howstuffworks.com/backhoe-loader.htm

Two of the many construction machines explained by the How Stuff Works people.

http://www.tallestskyscrapers.info/

The world's tallest buildings and how they were made.

Books

Big Machines (series), by David and Penny Glover, Franklin Watts, 2007

Extreme Machines: Trucks, by Ian Graham, Franklin Watts, 2006

How Machines Work: Construction Vehicles, by Terry Jennings, Franklin Watts, 2008

Mega Machine Drivers: This Is My Digger, by Chris Oxlade, Franklin Watts, 2006

Working Wheels (series), by Annabel Savery, Franklin Watts, 2010

Note to parents and teachers:

Every effort has been made by the Publishers to ensure that the websites in this book are suitable for children, that they are of the highest educational value, and that they contain no inappropriate or offensive material. However, because of the nature of the Internet, it is impossible to guarantee that the contents of these sites will not be altered. We strongly advise that Internet access is supervised by a responsible adult.

Index